SANKOFA
BLACK HERITAGE COLLECTION

FREEDOM

ADRIENNE SHADD

SERIES EDITOR • TOM HENDERSON

www.rubiconpublishing.com

Associate Publisher: Cheryl Turner
Project Editor: Jessica Rose
Editorial Assistant: Kaitlin Tremblay
Creative Director: Jennifer Drew
Graphic Designers: Roy Casim, Sherwin Flores, Robin Forsyth, Jennifer Harvey,
Stacy Jarvis, Jason Mitchell

Every reasonable effort has been made to trace the owners of copyrighted
material and to make due acknowledgement. Any errors or omissions
drawn to our attention will be gladly rectified in future editions.

14 15 16 17 18   5 4 3 2 1

ISBN: 978-1-77058-831-8

CONTENTS

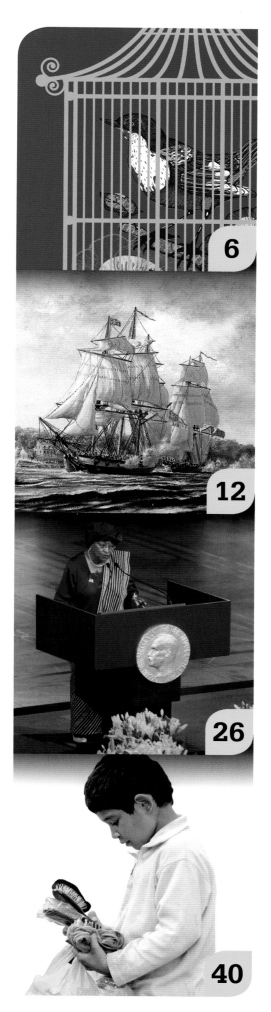

FREEDOM

Freedom is about self-determination. It means being able to make your own decisions and take your life in whatever direction you want it to go.

Throughout history, some people have had to fight for freedom — the freedom to have basic human rights, such as freedom of speech, freedom of association, freedom of religion, and freedom to choose their government. Sometimes, the battle is waged peacefully through words and peaceful resistance. Other times, fighting for freedom results in conflicts, revolutions, wars, and, sadly, loss of life.

Why are people willing to fight for freedom?

CagedBird

BY MAYA ANGELOU

THINK ABOUT IT

With a partner, talk about how the title "Caged Bird" makes you feel. What do you think the poem might be about?

A free bird leaps
on the back of the wind
and floats downstream
till the current ends
and dips his wing
in the orange sun rays
and dares to claim the sky.

But a bird that stalks
down his narrow cage
can seldom see through
his bars of rage
his wings are clipped and
his feet are tied
so he opens his throat to sing.

ABOUT THE POET

The African American writer Maya Angelou is one of the world's most beloved writers. She is a poet, screenwriter, novelist, educator, and activist. She has received over 30 honorary degrees as well as the American Presidential Medal of Arts and the Lincoln Medal.

The caged bird sings
with a fearful trill
of things unknown
but longed for still
and his tune is heard
on the distant hill
for the caged bird
sings of freedom.

The free bird thinks of another breeze
and the trade winds soft through the sighing trees
and the fat worms waiting on a dawn-bright lawn
and he names the sky his own.

But a caged bird stands on the grave of dreams
his shadow shouts on a nightmare scream
his wings are clipped and his feet are tied
so he opens his throat to sing.

The caged bird sings
with a fearful trill
of things unknown
but longed for still
and his tune is heard
on the distant hill
for the caged bird
sings of freedom.

trill: *fluttering or unsteady sound, like that made by certain birds*

What are the differences between a caged bird and a free bird?

CONNECT IT

With a partner, choose one stanza of this poem and discuss what it means to you. How were your explanations the same? How were they different? What freedoms are important to you?

FIGHTING FOR FREEDOM:

MANY PEOPLE FOUGHT for freedom against slavery in North America. Fighting for freedom sometimes took the form of military action, such as fighting in wars like the American Civil War. However, some people fought for freedom simply by running away, by assisting others to escape, by organizing campaigns against slavery, by giving speeches, and by establishing anti-slavery newspapers. After slavery was abolished, people continued to fight against discrimination and inequality by choosing to peacefully resist unfair treatment. Read the following timeline to learn about fighting for freedom in North America.

This painting shows a ship carrying African captives to America.

An estimated 12 million African men, women, and children, mainly from West and Central Africa, are captured and transported across the ocean to slavery in North, Central, and South America. This brutal voyage becomes known as the "Middle Passage."

Slavery is practised in the British and French colonies of what is now Canada. A six-year-old boy from Madagascar is sold to a French Canadian. He is later given the name Olivier Le Jeune.

Shelburne, Nova Scotia, is the site of the first race riot in Canada. White soldiers feel that Black workers in the area are reducing the soldiers' opportunities for employment. Mobs of White people beat Black people in the streets and tear down the homes of many Black people.

1628

1784

1400s–1800s

1793

1783

1619

The British transport over 3000 Black Loyalists to Nova Scotia. Birchtown becomes the largest settlement of free Black people in North America. Black Loyalists are people of African descent who were loyal to the British Crown during the American Revolutionary War. They fought alongside the British for their freedom. They were soldiers and active participants in the war.

An enslaved woman in Queenston, Ontario, named Chloe Cooley is sold to someone in New York State. Her screams and struggle while being tied up and forced onto a boat lead Lieutenant-Governor John Graves Simcoe to pass *The Anti-Slavery Act of 1793*, limiting slavery in Upper Canada.

The first enslaved Africans land in Jamestown, Virginia.

From the Past to the Present

Emancipation Day parade near Windsor, Ontario, in the 1890s

Harriet Tubman escapes from slavery in Maryland. She returns many times to Maryland and other states where slavery exists to help bring family members, friends, and others to the northern United States and Canada.

Great Britain passes the *Abolition of the Slave Trade Act* on 25 March.

Slavery is ended in the British Empire, including Canada. Emancipation Day celebrations on 1 August begin in Black communities in Ontario and other parts of Canada.

Henry and Mary Bibb begin publishing the *Voice of the Fugitive* newspaper in Sandwich, Canada West (now Windsor, Ontario).

1807 — 1812-1815 — 1834 — 1837 — 1849 — 1850 — 1851

The War of 1812 breaks out between Great Britain and the United States in what will be modern-day Canada. A unit of Black soldiers known as the "Coloured Corps" helps fight against an American invasion. Approximately 2000 enslaved people gain their freedom in Nova Scotia when they flee behind British lines during the War of 1812.

The 1837 Rebellion begins in Upper and Lower Canada. Black volunteers form a number of Coloured Corps in Upper Canada, which help to end the rebellion.

Ontario's Chief Superintendent of Education Egerton Ryerson passes a law that creates separate schools for Black children. It forces Black children into segregated schools across Upper Canada.

segregated: *set apart from one another*

9

Mary Ann Shadd and Samuel Ringgold Ward print the first issue of the *Provincial Freeman* newspaper in Windsor, Ontario.

American President Abraham Lincoln issues the Emancipation Proclamation on 1 January.

The Brotherhood of Sleeping Car Porters is organized in Canada. It becomes the first all-Black union to sign a collective agreement with a Canadian company, CP Rail.

Men from the Brotherhood of Sleeping Car Porters in the 1930s

1853   **1863**   **1942**

1861   **1893**   **1916**   **1946**

School group in Ontario, between 1910 and 1930

Schools in Chatham, Ontario, are finally desegregated after a well-organized campaign led by the Kent County Civil Rights League.

The American Civil War begins. Canadian-born Dr. Anderson Ruffin Abbott is one of eight Black surgeons to serve during the Civil War. He is the first Canadian-born Black doctor.

During World War I, a separate No. 2 Construction Battalion is formed by Black men in Canada who were denied the right to serve. Over 600 men join from across Canada and the United States.

Carrie Best publishes *The Clarion* and fights for the rights and dignity of African Nova Scotians. Viola Desmond refuses to sit in the balcony reserved for Black people in a New Glasgow, Nova Scotia, theatre. She is arrested, jailed, and fined $20. She pays the fine but fights the charge in court. Carrie Best covers this story in *The Clarion*.

A Fair Employment Practices Committee (FEPC) press conference, 1942

The Government of Ontario passes the Fair Employment Practices Act after pressure from African Canadian and labour organizations. The act outlaws discrimination in employment based on race, religion, or national origin.

The last segregated school in Ontario is closed.

Governor General Michaëlle Jean greets schoolchildren, in Yellowknife, 2006.

Her Excellency the Right Honourable Michaëlle Jean is appointed Governor General of Canada. She is the first person of African descent to serve in the post.

The Ontario Human Rights Code is enacted. It is the first of its kind in Canada.

The last segregated school in Nova Scotia is closed.

1951

1962

1965

1983

2005

1948

1968

1993

THE UNIVERSAL DECLARATION OF Human Rights

The United Nations adopts the Universal Declaration of Human Rights, which says that all people are entitled to certain rights and freedoms regardless of race, colour, sex, religion, political opinion, national origin, birth, or other status.

Lincoln Alexander becomes the first Black Member of Parliament in Canada and goes on to become the first Lieutenant-Governor of Ontario of African descent.

The Honourable Jean Augustine is sworn in as the first Black woman elected to the Canadian Parliament.

CONNECT IT

This timeline highlights the various ways that different people have fought for freedom. With a partner, find out about other people or events that could be added to this timeline.

John "Daddy" Hall and the Detroit River Frontier

DURING THE WAR of 1812, African Canadians fought alongside British and First Nations troops. Among these soldiers was John Hall. Read about him in this article from the Harriet Tubman Institute for Research on the Global Migrations of African Peoples.

THINK ABOUT IT

With a partner, discuss major wars that you know about. Who were important people in these wars? What did they do?

Why would the First Nations people not want more European pioneers to settle in North America?

One of the reasons that the Americans declared war on Great Britain in 1812 was because they wanted more land for settlement in the western and northern parts of North America. First Nations peoples who were friendly with the British did not want more European pioneers living on their land, so they fought back in a series of skirmishes, battles, and raids on pioneer communities. The Americans were angry because they believed that the British helped the Native peoples in conducting these raids and supplied the guns and ammunition.

The War of 1812 started in June, and by July the American commander at Detroit, General William Hull, invaded Upper Canada. His troops crossed over the Detroit River to where Windsor, Ontario, is today, and took the town of Sandwich. But when Hull tried to take Fort Amherstburg, near the southern end of the Detroit River, he was pushed back. He and his troops returned to Detroit.

Even though the Americans had a much larger army, General Isaac Brock and his brilliant ally, the Shawnee Chief Tecumseh, tricked General Hull into believing there were far more men on the British Canadian side than there really were. General Hull surrendered on 16 August 1812.

There were African Canadians fighting in several military units with British and First Nations troops. For instance, a man named John Hall served as a scout for Chief Tecumseh. John Hall lost his whole family and his freedom because he fought in the War of 1812. John had 12 brothers and sisters. They lived on the Canadian side of the Detroit River

---

skirmishes: *brief, unplanned small outbursts of fighting among soldiers*

John "Daddy" Hall

between Sandwich and Amherstburg, and were the children of a Mohawk father and an African mother. John Hall fought at the Battle of Stoney Creek, where he was wounded. When he returned home, the American troops took him, his mother, and uncle, and all 12 of the Hall children as prisoners of war. They were carried off to Virginia. At the end of the war, the whole family was sold as slaves to different owners. John Hall never saw any member of his family again.

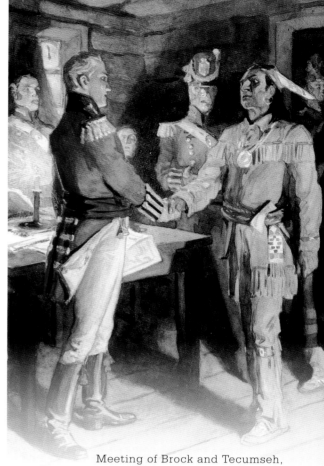

Meeting of Brock and Tecumseh, by C.W. Jeffreys

John Hall lost his whole family and his freedom because he fought in the War of 1812.

John Hall was sent to live in Kentucky as a slave. He eventually escaped on the Underground Railroad. When he came to Canada, he first lived in Toronto. Eventually, John Hall and his wife, Esther, migrated north to Owen Sound, on Georgian Bay. They started a farm, cleared the land, and built a log cabin. John Hall was over 60 years old by this time, but he wanted a new life for himself and his children.

Why do you think he wanted a new life for his children in Canada?

The town of Owen Sound needed a town crier. In the days before radio, television, or the Internet, this was a man who went about town ringing a bell and telling everyone the day's news. John Hall was the town crier for many, many years. This Black veteran of the War of 1812 died in Owen Sound, Ontario, in 1900. He was 117 years old.

CONNECT IT

Using the Internet, research other African Canadian soldiers who helped to keep Canada a free land. Create a hero card for this person, explaining why his or her fight for freedom was important to Canada.

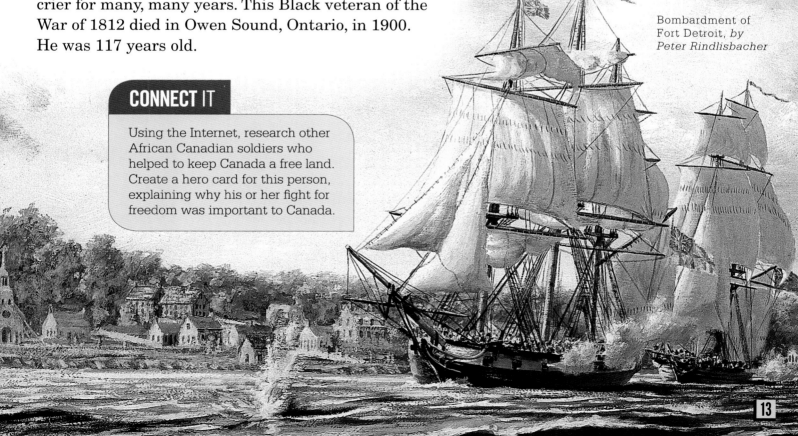

Bombardment of Fort Detroit, by Peter Rindlisbacher

HIRED OUT

BY AFUA COOPER

THINK ABOUT IT

Imagine being nine years old and spending your day working without getting paid. How would you feel? Discuss with a partner.

Portrait of Henry Bibb, 1854

"HIRED OUT" IS an excerpt from a fictionalized biographical novel called *My Name is Henry Bibb: A Story of Slavery and Freedom*, by Afua Cooper. Henry Bibb was a real person. His mother was enslaved on a plantation in Kentucky. She worked in the house of the owner of the plantation. At the age of nine, Henry was hired out by his owner to work on another plantation. One day, he heard other workers singing a song about a place called Canada. While the events in this novel really happened, Cooper fictionalized them for literary impact.

Fall came and with it cooler weather. It was the time of harvest. Though the widow did not approve of house slaves socializing with those who worked in the field, I would go down to the slave quarters whenever my work allowed, and I quickly got to know the slave folks who lived there. One evening in late October, I went to play with a boy my age named David. The adults were preparing for a corn-shucking. David and I walked out to the cornfields with them. Shucking corn was work but also a time of merrymaking, and the sociability made the work seem lighter. Slaves from neighbouring farms would join in the harvest, moving between farms to pick and store the crops.

Slaveowners gave permission for the shucking, but it was the slave people who organized it. About 50 slaves assembled at the cornfield. … They chose captains and divided themselves into three groups. Each group would try to shuck its row of corn faster than the other two. As the men and women broke down the dried cornstalks, removed the outer leaves of the corn, took the corn from its stalk, removed the silk, and then threw the corn in wooden bins at the end of each path, they lifted their voices in song.

The captain called and his workers answered.

Captain: *Fare you well, Miss Lucy*
All: *John come down to de hollow*
Captain: *Fare you well, fare you well*
All: *Well ooh, well ooh*
Captain: *Fare you well, young ladies all*

ABOUT THE AUTHOR

Dr. Afua Cooper is a historian specializing in the areas of slavery and abolition. She is the James R. Johnston Chair in Black Canadian Studies at Dalhousie University as well as an award-winning author and poet. She specializes in researching and writing about early African Canadian communities and the people who lived in them.

Corn-shucking on a farm in Granville County, North Carolina

All: *Well ooh, well ooh*
Captain: *Fare you well all, I'm going away*
All: *Well ooh, well ooh*
Captain: *I'm going away to Canada*
All: *Well ooh, well ooh!*

The song had a mournful air even though the people sang it with powerful voices. I knew the song well but had never really paid attention to the words. Now, as the people sang, I heard "I'm going away to Canada" as if for the first time. The words went around in my head. But what is Canada? It must be a place, but where? I knew of Tennessee, Ohio, Indiana, and such, but I did not know of that place. I asked David, but he said he did not know either.

That night as I helped Elliot polish the silver, I asked him.

"Where did you hear that, boy?" he asked harshly.

"From the corn-shucking song."

"Oh," he said, and remained quiet for a while.

Then he said, "It's a free place way up north. Another country, not America. They have a king. They speak English like us. Many slave people from Kentucky go there."

> Songs were often used to carry messages of freedom. What other songs do you know that are about freedom?

"Ohio and Indiana are free places," I ventured.

"Yes, but a massa can still go there and capture runaways. It's safer to head straight to Canada." Elliot stopped polishing and looked off into space. After a while he added, "Or Mexico."

"Where is that?"

"Way south. They speak Spanish there."

"But there is no slavery there?"

"No."

"How do you get there?"

"Mexico?"

"No. Canada."

"You cross the Ohio River to a free state and keep on very far north." Elliot took up his polishing rag again but looked directly at me. "Now, Henry, don't go asking too many questions, you hear?"

massa: *variation of master*

VOICE OF THE FUGITIVE.

Voice of the Fugitive
*Vol. I No. 6, printed
on 12 March 1851*

Henry Bibb escaped to freedom in Cincinnati, Ohio, in 1837, but he was recaptured. A few years later, he escaped again and made it to Detroit, Michigan. Bibb spent the next few years making speeches against slavery and, around 1849, he published his autobiography.

In 1850, he moved to Canada, where he founded the first newspaper for African Canadians, called *Voice of the Fugitive*. Bibb was active in the anti-slavery movement in Canada. He worked with Josiah Henson to form the Refugees' Home Colony for people who had escaped enslavement.

CONNECT IT

Write a short speech or newspaper article about why slavery is wrong. Include examples from this story and other things you have read.

Stand Up and Be Counted

THINK ABOUT IT

What does the phrase "stand up and be counted" mean? Brainstorm different ways you can stand up against discrimination in your daily life.

VIOLA DESMOND IS an important figure in the fight for freedom in Canada because she refused to move to the segregated "coloured" section of a movie theatre. Read the following reader's theatre script and learn about Viola Desmond, along with Lauren, Tyrone, and Kiera.

CHARACTERS:

- **Narrator**
- **Grandma**
- **Lauren, aged 12**
- **Tyrone, aged 10**
- **Kiera, aged 6**

Narrator: Lauren, Tyrone, and Kiera are playing tag in the backyard at their grandmother's house. Trying to get away from Tyrone, Lauren runs behind a large chestnut tree and scrapes her arm on the bark of the tree. Bleeding from the cut, Lauren rushes into the house to her grandmother.

Lauren *(running to her grandmother):* Grandma! I cut myself. Can you get me a bandage, please?

Grandma *(peering over her glasses as she examines something):* Okay, sweetheart, let's see.

Narrator: Grandma leaves the room and returns with a first-aid kit. She bandages Lauren's arm quickly.

Grandma: There you go. Feel better now?

Lauren: Yes. Thank you! … Whatcha doin', Grandma?

Grandma: Oh, just looking at some old newspaper clippings. My dad saved them. This one is about Viola Desmond. She was a woman who made history … and she was from right here in Halifax.

Lauren: What'd she do, Grandma?

Grandma: Well, she did what my daddy always said you should do — stand up and be counted. She refused to be treated as a second-class citizen.

Lauren (looking at a clipping): But what exactly did she do?

Narrator: Tyrone and Kiera run into the room looking for Lauren.

Tyrone (looking frustrated): Lauren, what's taking so long? We're supposed to be playing tag.

Grandma: I was just giving your sister a bandage and telling her about an important woman who was told she had to sit upstairs in the balcony of a movie theatre because she was Black. You see, they wouldn't allow her to sit downstairs on the main floor to watch the movie. Can you imagine that? And you know what she did? She refused to move upstairs to the "coloured" section of the movie theatre. And for that, she made history!

Viola Desmond

Kiera *(innocently):*
> What's the big deal about sitting downstairs at the movies, anyway? We all sit downstairs.

Lauren *(eyes wide in disbelief):*
> She couldn't sit where she wanted to just because she was Black? And it happened here in Halifax?

Grandma: Well, actually, it happened in New Glasgow, but yes, that's right. Black folks weren't allowed to sit downstairs at the movies in some places in Nova Scotia. As I was saying, she refused to move upstairs, and guess what? They arrested her and she spent the night in jail.

Tyrone: What year was this, Grandma?

Grandma: This happened in 1946.

Tyrone: Back in the olden days …

Grandma *(twisting her mouth and pretending to be insulted):*
> It wasn't that long ago. I was just a child, but I remember my parents talking about it. My mother used to get her hair done at Mrs. Desmond's beauty parlour, and we were friends of the family. In any case, Mrs. Desmond was taken to the police station and thrown in jail.

Lauren: And what happened after that?

Grandma: Well, there was a trial the next day, and she was convicted of some bogus offence — wait a minute … it's right here — she was convicted of not paying the extra one cent in tax it cost to sit downstairs. They pretended that her race had nothing to do with it.

Kiera: Can we go out and play now?

Lauren *(ignoring her sister):*
> So that's why she's so famous?

Grandma: Well, yes … but also because she appealed her conviction. Lawsuits cost a lot of money. A group called the Nova Scotia Association for the Advancement of Coloured People raised money and let people know about the case. And Carrie Best wrote about it in her newspaper called *The Clarion*. So it was well known around Nova Scotia that there was this Black woman who had the guts to fight racism. You see, Black people at that time were discriminated against in many ways.

Lauren: That's not fair! Why didn't more people do something about it?

Grandma: Some people felt that we were making slow progress, and you shouldn't rock the boat. But Viola Desmond understood that we should fight these indignities rather than just accept them year after year.

Lauren: Did she win her case?

Grandma: No, unfortunately, she didn't. But the point is that she fought for her rights and her dignity. ◀

> Why is fighting for fair treatment important, even if you lose the fight?

Lauren: And that's why she's so important.

Grandma: That's right, dear.

Kiera *(impatiently):*
Can we go now?

Grandma: Yes, Kiera. But you might be interested to know that, in 2010, the Government of Nova Scotia apologized to Mrs. Desmond and pardoned her, 45 years after she had passed away. And I just want to finish by saying that Viola Desmond is now very important in Canadian history because she wasn't afraid to stand up and be counted.

Tyrone: And now you better stand up and count while I run out that door. Last one out is a rotten eeeggggg!!!!

CONNECT IT

Research another Canadian woman who dared to stand up and be counted. Write a blog post describing what she stood up for. Remember to answer the 5 Ws and H: who, what, where, when, why, and how.

EMANCIPATION DAY MEMORIES

THINK ABOUT IT

What is your favourite memory about living in Canada? What makes it a special Canadian memory?

North Buxton Maple Leaf Band passing the grandstand at the Windsor Emancipation Day parade, 1965

EVERY YEAR, MANY Canadians celebrate the first of August. This day is called Emancipation Day. Emancipation Day marks the day in August in 1834 when slavery ended throughout the British Empire. Since that time, this date has been observed by Black communities across Canada, and continues to be celebrated in Ontario. As a young girl, Adrienne Shadd marched as a majorette in the Windsor, Ontario, Emancipation Day parade. In this memoir, she writes about her experiences.

As a child, I marched in Emancipation Day celebrations in Windsor, Ontario, in the early 1960s. I was a majorette in the North Buxton Maple Leaf Band, led by Ira Shadd. Our band was well known. We were invited to perform in many parades and events. Uncle Ira, as I called him (although he was actually my third cousin), was the founder of the band. He was a musical genius. He taught everyone how to play his or her instrument. My dad, Thomas, was the drum major. The drum major marched at the front of the band, leading it. Dad was tall and had a regal, dignified air that impressed many people. The man could strut. The rest of the band members were mostly residents of Buxton. There were relatives from as far away as Detroit, Cincinnati, and even New York City who also played in the band. We had a corps of crack drummers who kept a tight rhythm. One of the pieces we often played was "The Maple Leaf Forever." Michael Bublé sang this march song during the closing ceremonies of the Winter Olympics in Vancouver, British Columbia, in 2010.

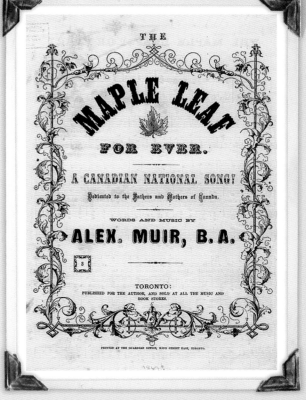

The original cover to the sheet music for the song "The Maple Leaf Forever," printed in 1868

"The Maple Leaf Forever" was written in 1867 to celebrate Canada's Confederation. Why is it important that it was sung in Emancipation Day celebrations and at the Olympics?

With as many as 100 000 spectators, the Saturday parade was Windsor's biggest annual show. In its day, it was one of the biggest in Canada.

In the 1960s, Windsor's Emancipation Day weekend was the biggest Emancipation celebration in Ontario. As one of the few African Canadian bands — and a good one at that — we were invited to march in the Saturday parade. With as many as 100 000 spectators, the Saturday parade was Windsor's biggest annual show. In its day, it was one of the biggest in Canada. As a child, I remember the huge crowds gathered along the parade route, especially once we reached the main street in downtown Windsor. It was thrilling to be part of the spectacle. When relatives or friends saw us coming, they would clap and shout our name. "Yaaaaay, North Buxton!! Way to go North Buxton … Yaaaaay!!!"

regal: *like a king or queen; impressive*

What set this parade apart, however, was that the majority of the participants were of African heritage. This made it quite unusual for a parade of this size in a Canadian city.

Besides our band, there were dozens of other marching bands, floats, precision marchers, clowns, motorcycle teams, and important people in the parade. The Miss Sepia beauty contestants, dozens of local dark-skinned beauties, waved from floats that wound through the parade route. The thing that stands out most in my memory was the African American drill units dressed in military uniforms and toting rifles. I remember being in awe of these handsome young men. They would chant things like "Sound off, one, two/Sound off, three, four/ Sound off, one, two, three, four." In many ways, they were like modern-day steppers. They were so rhythmic and exact in their drills and routines.

The parade was integrated in the sense that all-Black bands strutted alongside all-White ones. The onlookers included people of every nationality. What set this parade apart, however, was that the majority of the participants were of African heritage. This made it quite unusual for a parade of its size in a Canadian city. It had a soulful element that could not be denied. This, as I later learned, had a lot to do with a man named Walt Perry. He was behind the Windsor event. He would travel all around scouting bands and entertainers to bring to the celebrations. He made all the arrangements for these groups to appear. Not surprisingly, he was known as "Mr. Emancipation."

> Why would Walt Perry's commitment to making the parades a hit earn him the nickname "Mr. Emancipation"?

---

soulful: *full of or showing deep feeling*

The parade ended in Jackson Park, where midway rides and a huge barbecue pit were set up. You could buy and eat barbecued spareribs and chicken to your heart's content. Unfortunately, the only thing I remember is being loaded up into the car to return home. My Emancipation Day celebrations were brought to an abrupt end.

I never heard the speeches from Martin Luther King Jr., United States Congressman Adam Clayton Powell, or former First Lady Eleanor Roosevelt. I missed out on the talent shows and Miss Sepia beauty contests. I don't even think I got to taste the delicious barbecue. I just remember the great spectacle that was the parade, and the huge crowds that came out to see us. To my young mind, it certainly lived up to its billing: "the greatest freedom show on Earth."

abrupt: *sudden; unexpected*

(Left to Right) Bandleader Ira Shadd, Cecil Brooks, drum major Thomas Shadd, and majorette Adrienne Shadd

CONNECT IT

Explain in your own words why the Emancipation Day parade was called the "greatest freedom show on Earth." Do you think parades are an important part of fighting for freedom? Explain your answer.

FINDING YOUR VOICE

From left to right: 2011 Nobel Peace Prize winners Tawakkol Karman, Leymah Gbowee, and Ellen Johnson Sirleaf

THINK ABOUT IT

With a partner, list three places around the world where there have been revolutions or wars in the past few years. Discuss what might have caused these conflicts.

THE NOBEL PEACE Prize is awarded every year to a person or an organization that has made a major contribution to bringing peace to some place in the world. In 2011, the prize was shared by three African women. They were Ellen Johnson Sirleaf of Liberia, Leymah Gbowee of Liberia, and Tawakkol Karman of Yemen. At that time, Johnson Sirleaf was the president of Liberia. Liberia suffered from a civil war that started in the late 1980s. Approximately 250 000 people were killed in the civil war, which lasted until 2003. Johnson Sirleaf was named president in 2006 in the first election after the civil war ended. The following is an excerpt from Johnson Sirleaf's Nobel Peace Prize acceptance speech.

On behalf of all the women of Liberia, the women of Africa, and women everywhere in the world who have struggled for peace, justice, and equality, I accept with great humility the 2011 Nobel Prize for Peace.

I am particularly honoured to be a successor to the several sons and one daughter of Africa who have stood on this stage — Chief Albert John Lutuli, Archbishop Desmond Tutu, Nelson Mandela and F.W. de Klerk, Kofi Annan, Anwar el-Sadat, Wangari Muta Maathai, Mohamed ElBaradei, as well as Barack Obama, Martin Luther King Jr., and Ralph Bunche — Americans of African descent. ...

History will judge us not by what we say in this moment in time, but by what we do next to lift the lives of our countrymen and women.

I would like to take a moment to honour the memory of the late Wangari Maathai [of Kenya], the first African woman to receive this great honour. Her accomplishments will forever inspire us.

Accepting the award in December 2004, Professor Maathai said, "Those of us who have been privileged to receive education, skills, and experiences, and even power must be role models for the next generation of leadership!" May we all resolve to fulfill that duty!

> A role model is somebody who can be looked up to. Who are some of your role models?

I also honour the memory of countless women whose efforts and sacrifice will never be recognized, but who, in their private and silent struggles, helped to shape our world.

As Leymah and Tawakkol know, this award belongs to the people whose aspirations we have the privilege to represent, and whose rights we have the obligation to defend. We are but their reflection.

With such a distinction comes great responsibility. History will judge us not by what we say in this moment in time, but by what we do next to lift the lives of our countrymen and women. It will judge us by the legacy we leave behind for generations to come.

Tawakkol, you are an inspirational activist for peace and women's rights. In your country, autocratic rule prevails; but where they had no voice, you found a way to be heard.

Leymah, you are a peacemaker. You had the courage to mobilize the women of Liberia to take back their country. You redefined the "front line" of a brutal civil conflict — women dressed in white, demonstrating in the streets — a barrier no warlord was brave enough to cross.

---

autocratic: *relating to a ruler who has absolute power*

Mine has been a long journey, a lifetime journey to Oslo. It was shaped by the values of my parents and by my two grandmothers — indigenous Liberians — farmers and market traders, neither of whom could read or write. They taught me that only through service is one's life truly blessed.

My journey was supported by my many teachers and mentors who guided me to a world opened up by the enlightenment of higher education ... which led to my conviction that access to quality education is the social justice issue of our time.

My life was safeguarded when thousands mobilized around the world to free me from imprisonment, and my life was spared by individual acts of compassion by some of my captors.

My life was forever transformed when I was given the privilege to serve the people of Liberia — taking on the awesome responsibility of rebuilding a nation nearly destroyed by war and plunder. There was no road map for post-conflict transformation. But we knew that we could not let our country slip back into the past. We understood that our greatest responsibility was to keep the peace.

Your Majesties, my sisters and my brothers:

The Nobel Committee cannot license us three Laureates to speak for women. But it has provided us a platform from which to speak to women around the globe, whatever their nationality, their colour, their religion, or their station in life. It is you, my sisters ... to whom I dedicate my remarks, and this prize. ...

Today, across the globe, women, and also men, from all walks of life are finding the courage to say, loudly and firmly, in a thousand languages, "No more."

Ellen Johnson Sirleaf delivers her Nobel Peace Prize acceptance speech.

As we celebrate today, we are mindful of the enormous challenges we still face. In too many parts of the world, crimes against women are still under-reported, and the laws protecting women are under-enforced. In this 21st century, surely there is no place for human trafficking that victimizes almost a million people, mostly girls and women, each year. Surely there is no place for girls and women to be beaten and abused. Surely there is no place for a continuing belief that leadership qualities belong to only one gender.

Yet, there is occasion for optimism and hope. There are good signs of progress and change. Around the world, slowly, international law and an awareness of human rights are illuminating dark corners, in schools, in courts, in the marketplace.

The windows of closed chambers where men and women have been unspeakably abused are being opened. … The light is coming in. Democracies, even if tentatively, are taking root in lands unaccustomed to freedom.

As curtains are raised and as the sun shines upon dark places, what was previously invisible comes into view. Technology has turned our world into one interconnected neighbourhood. What happens in one place is seen in every corner. … There has been no better time for the spread of peace, democracy, and their attending social justice and fairness for all.

Today, across the globe, women, and also men, from all walks of life are finding the courage to say, loudly and firmly, in a thousand languages, "No more." They reject mindless violence, and defend the fundamental values of democracy, of open society, of freedom, and of peace.

So I urge my sisters, and my brothers, not to be afraid. Be not afraid to denounce injustice, though you may be outnumbered. Be not afraid to seek peace, even if your voice may be small. Be not afraid to demand peace.

If I might thus speak to girls and women everywhere, I would issue them this simple invitation: My sisters, my daughters, my friends, find your voices!

Each of us has her own voice, and the differences among us are to be celebrated. But our goals are in harmony. They are the pursuit of peace, the pursuit of justice. They are the defence of rights to which all people are entitled.

The political struggles that our countries, Liberia, Yemen, and others, have gone through will be meaningful only if the new-found freedom opens new opportunities for all. We are well aware that a new order, born of hunger for change, can easily fall back into the lawless ways of the past. We need our voices to be heard. Find your voice! And raise your voice! Let yours be a voice for freedom!

Women and men at a campaign rally for Johnson Sirleaf in Monrovia, Liberia, 6 August 2011

CONNECT IT

Research the speech of another woman who has won the Nobel Peace Prize. You could choose somebody mentioned in this piece. Practise her speech and present it in your class.

FREE

THINK ABOUT IT

What, if anything, would you risk your freedom for? Share examples of people you know from history who have risked their freedom for something they believe in.

FEW PEOPLE UNDERSTAND the importance of freedom as Nelson Mandela did. The man who became the first Black president of South Africa spent 27 years in prison. He was imprisoned for fighting for basic human rights for the Black people of his country. People all over the world mourned when he died in 2013.

Mandela addresses a crowd on 5 September 1990.

MANDELA!

Nelson Mandela was born on 18 July 1918 in a village called Mvezo on the Mbashe River in South Africa. When Mandela was a child, his family moved to a nearby village called Qunu. In his autobiography, Mandela recalls his childhood as a time of happiness. However, his family faced hardship, too. His father, Gadla Henry Mphakanyiswa, died of lung disease when Mandela was only nine.

Mandela took his education seriously. In 1943, he enrolled at the University of the Witwatersrand in Johannesburg to study law. Witwatersrand was one of the few universities in South Africa that accepted Black students.

Life for Black people in South Africa was not easy. White South Africans held almost all the economic and political power. Mandela, along with many of his friends, joined the African National Congress (ANC). He helped form the ANC Youth League, which organized protests against racial discrimination.

Life became even more difficult for Black South Africans in 1948. In that year, South Africa's government, led by the National Party, introduced Apartheid. The word "Apartheid" means "apartness" in Afrikaans.

Afrikaans: *language of Dutch origin that is spoken in a number of countries, including South Africa*

In 1994, Mandela visited one of the cells in which he was confined for 27 years.

Under Apartheid, non-White people were forced to live their lives segregated from White people. Non-White and White people were no longer allowed to mix in public places. Mixed-race marriage was illegal. Black South Africans even had to live in separate communities. Living conditions in Black communities, called townships, were not as good as in other South African communities. The government did not provide people with adequate housing, water, hospitals, or schools in the townships. Black communities were so overcrowded that up to 20 people had to live in one small house.

Nelson Mandela and the ANC joined the fight against Apartheid by organizing protests and boycotts of businesses. The ANC encouraged Black South Africans to break the Apartheid laws by going into areas where they were not allowed.

In 1962, Mandela, along with many other leaders of the ANC, was arrested and charged with sabotage against the government. After a long trial, he was sentenced to life imprisonment and sent to Robben Island prison. Robben Island was known as the toughest prison in South Africa. Strong currents in the water around the island made it difficult to escape.

Nelson Mandela and the ANC preferred non-violent protests, but sometimes advocated violence if non-violence did not work. Do you think there is ever room for violence in activism? Why or why not?

While imprisoned on Robben Island, Nelson Mandela and the other prisoners were required to do hard labour. Prisoners spent hours in the hot sun breaking up rocks into gravel.

Even in prison, men were segregated by race. Black prisoners were given less food and fewer supplies than White prisoners. Mandela was allowed only one visitor a year. He rarely saw his wife, Winnie, or his children. Mandela was not even allowed to attend the funeral of his mother, Noqaphi Nosekeni, or eldest son, Madiba Thembekile.

Even though he had his freedom taken from him, Mandela didn't give up fighting for the rights of others. He became a leader in the prison community. He demanded better living conditions, including better food, for prisoners.

Why do you think Mandela took on these causes?

Outside the prison, Black South Africans and their White allies were continuing the fight against Apartheid. Mandela found ways to communicate with Black leaders outside the prison. He wrote coded messages on toilet paper and had people smuggle them out of the prison. A released prisoner helped by smuggling out Mandela's memoirs so that the world could read his story.

> **Even though he had his freedom taken from him, Mandela didn't give up fighting for the rights of others. He became a leader in the prison community.**

Countries around the world were demanding that the South African government release Mandela. Many countries, including Canada, introduced sanctions against South Africa. This meant they would not buy or trade any products or resources with South Africa until the country ended Apartheid. In 1986, the United States Congress passed a law that banned South African Airlines from landing airplanes anywhere in the United States.

The South African government realized that they faced an economic crisis if Apartheid was not ended and Mandela was not freed. Mandela was finally released from prison in 1990. He had spent 27 years in jail.

Tens of thousands of people greeted Mandela in the days after his release. Many people danced in the streets and threw huge celebrations in his honour. Following his release, Mandela worked with South Africa's new president, F.W. de Klerk, to improve living conditions for Black South Africans. The two men shared the Nobel Peace Prize in 1993.

That same year, Nelson Mandela ran for president of South Africa. This was the first time Black South Africans were allowed to vote in a national election. Mandela won the election. He was sworn in as the country's first Black president on 10 May 1994. He was 75 years old.

As president, Mandela oversaw the development of a new constitution for South Africa. This constitution gave the same rights to all South Africans. He also helped establish the Truth and Reconciliation Commission. Archbishop Desmond Tutu led the commission. It investigated the atrocities that happened during Apartheid. Mandela retired from the presidency in 1999. He was 81 years old.

In 2001, Nelson Mandela became an honorary Canadian citizen. The Canadian government granted him citizenship to recognize his "great moral leadership to South Africa and to all humanity."

Mandela died at the age of 95 on 5 December 2013. Over 80 000 people attended a mass tribute to him in the FNB Stadium in the Soweto area of Johannesburg, South Africa.

< What rights do you believe all people should have?

CONNECT IT

Mandela is not the only leader who has had to sacrifice his or her freedom to fight for the rights of others. Use the Web and other resources to learn about other freedom fighters. Research and write a short biography of another person who fought for freedom.

---

atrocities: *cruel acts, especially involving physical violence*

A crowd gathers at Orlando Stadium, South Africa, in February 1990 to catch a glimpse of Mandela and to celebrate his release.

PEACEFUL PROTEST

THINK ABOUT IT

With a partner, write a pro and con list about using non-violent ways of fighting for freedom.

A famous peaceful protest in the 1950s was the Montgomery Bus Boycott. African Americans boycotted buses after Rosa Parks was arrested for not giving up her seat on a bus.

The March on Washington is where Martin Luther King Jr. delivered his famous "I Have A Dream" speech. It inspired Americans to continue fighting for equality.

Nelson Mandela and Martin Luther King Jr. never met, but both fought similar battles against racism and discrimination. King was a leader in the American Civil Rights Movement. He fought against racial discrimination in the 1950s and 1960s. After slavery was abolished, many African Americans still faced prejudice. In some places, African Americans could not even eat in the same restaurants as White Americans.

> Martin Luther King Jr. led many peaceful fights for equality. His peaceful resistance included protests, boycotts, singing songs, and marches. In 1961, King was arrested during a protest in Albany, Georgia. Peaceful protests were happening in Canada, too, by people like Viola Desmond.

> The March on Washington on 28 August 1963 was a peaceful protest led by Martin Luther King Jr. He believed that non-violent protests were necessary to fight against discrimination.

abolished: *officially ended by law*

Black and White demonstrators during the March on Washington

CONNECT IT

In a large group, pick an issue to protest. Brainstorm a peaceful protest against something you think is unfair.

AIN'T GONNA LET NOBODY TURN ME AROUND

THINK ABOUT IT

Why are songs a good way to build support in a community? With a partner, discuss other songs that are about community.

"AIN'T GONNA LET Nobody Turn Me Around" is a popular song of the Civil Rights Movement. It is a traditional American song. Traditional and gospel songs were often sung during the Civil Rights Movement. They were simple and powerful and anybody could learn to sing them. "Ain't Gonna Let Nobody Turn Me Around" is about refusing to give up fighting for freedom.

As you read the lyrics, think about how repeating short phrases can be powerful.

> Ain't gonna let nobody turn me around
Turn me around, turn me around
Ain't gonna let nobody turn me around
I'm gonna keep on a-walkin', keep on a-talkin'
Marchin' up to freedom land.

Ain't gonna let no injunction turn me around
Turn me around, turn me around
Ain't gonna let no injunction turn me around
I'm gonna keep on a-walkin', keep on a-talkin'
Marchin' up to freedom land.

---

injunction: *court order explaining what can and cannot be done*

Ain't gonna let no hatred turn me around
Turn me around, turn me around
Ain't gonna let no hatred turn me around
I'm gonna keep on a-walkin', keep on a-talkin'
Marchin' up to freedom land.

Ain't gonna let racism turn me around
Turn me around, turn me around
Ain't gonna let racism turn me around
I'm gonna keep on a-walkin', keep on a-talkin'
Marchin' up to freedom land.

Ain't gonna let injustice turn me around
Turn me around, turn me around
Ain't gonna let injustice turn me around
I'm gonna keep on a-walkin', keep on a-talkin'
Marchin' up to freedom land.

Ain't gonna let no jail cell turn me around
Turn me around, turn me around
Ain't gonna let no jail cell turn me around
I'm gonna keep on a-walkin', keep on a-talkin'
Marchin' up to freedom land.

Ain't gonna let nobody turn me around
Turn me around, turn me around
Ain't gonna let nobody turn me around
I'm gonna keep on a-walkin', keep on a-talkin'
Marchin' up to freedom land.

CONNECT IT

With a small group, write a song to help someone overcome an obstacle. As a group, decide what the obstacle is and the best ways to overcome it.

A musical band from the No.2 Construction Battalion, 1917

LIBERATION FORCES

THINK ABOUT IT

Why might African Canadians have wanted to fight in World War I and World War II?

WHEN CANADA JOINED World War I as part of Britain's Allied Forces, many African Canadian men wanted to enlist. However, some White soldiers didn't want to serve with Black soldiers. For two years, Black men kept trying to enlist. Finally, on 5 July 1916, a new battalion was formed. It was called the No. 2 Construction Battalion.

The No. 2 Construction Battalion cut lumber, built shelters, and dug trenches. The soldiers played a crucial role in the war effort even though they did not fight on the front lines. When World War II erupted in Europe in 1939, it was easier for Black men to enlist. While there was still some segregation, many Black Canadians fought alongside White Canadians. Women contributed to the war effort by serving as nurses and working in factories.

The father of Canadian writer Clifton Ruggles was one of the hundreds of African Canadian soldiers who fought during World War II. In the following personal account, he tells about sharing Remembrance Day with his father at Dominion Square in Montreal, Quebec.

Two soldiers play a game of bingo on board their ship during World War II.

Remembrance Day always brings me back to rainy Novembers when my father would take us down to Dominion Square to commemorate the lost lives of his comrades-in-arms.

When he donned his poppy and veteran's pin, he seemed to stand taller than I ever remembered him.

Shivering from the cold, I would move closer to him for warmth. He put his strong hands firmly on my shoulder, pressing me closer to him. His pride was my pride.

I remember the preparations for that day. Each of us would have to shine our shoes, to have what he referred to as a "spit-polish shine." When you look at that shoe, you should be able to see the reflection of your face. And if you didn't, he'd make you do it again. He'd take a quarter out of his pocket and drop it on one of our beds. If it bounced, we passed inspection.

Everyone understood the importance of these ceremonial proceedings. When the final preparations were concluded, when every shirt was tucked in, every button done up, and ties so tight you felt as if you were about to choke, we were ready to embark on our trip to Dominion Square. Beaming with pride, I'd ask him, "Dad, how do I look?" And he'd reply, "Sharp as a tack and twice as dangerous." Then, like soldiers on parade, he'd march all nine of us children out the door.

My father's wartime experiences were very positive. He was very proud of being part of the liberation forces. He felt it was among the few times he, as a Black man, was regarded as a human being, and I guess that's why he wanted to remember it.

Most of my dad's life was spent experiencing rejection and discrimination. Suddenly, for the first time in his life, thousands of White faces welcomed him as he marched through towns in Europe as part of the liberation troops.

> Why do you think Clifton Ruggles's father wanted to share this experience with his children?

CONNECT IT

Imagine you are interviewing Clifton Ruggles's father. Write five questions you would ask him about his wartime experiences.

LIVING IN SLAVERY

SLAVERY TODAY

The United Nations 1948 Universal Declaration of Human Rights prohibits slavery. The rights outlined in the declaration are supposed to apply to all human beings. Unfortunately, this has not stopped slavery around the world. An estimated 12 to 30 million people are imprisoned in slavery around the world today.

According to Anti-Slavery International, people are enslaved if they experience the following:

- being forced by threats to work
- being "owned" by someone acting as an employer
- being dehumanized or treated ◀ as property
- having their movement restricted or being constrained

To dehumanize someone is to treat the person with a lack of the respect that every human deserves.

---

constrained: *limited*

A child working on the streets

FORMS OF MODERN-DAY SLAVERY

Here are some forms of slavery that Anti-Slavery International outlines as still existing today:

- **Bonded labour:** People are forced or tricked into taking money that they can never repay. They are then forced into bonded labour to pay off the debt. Although this happens around the world, most people forced into bonded labour live in Southeast Asia.

> While Southeast Asia faces very high numbers of modern-day slavery, the trafficking of people is a major problem in Eastern Europe and North America.

- **Forced labour:** People are illegally made to work under the threat of violence. The threat can be against themselves or their loved ones.
- **Descent-based slavery:** People are born into a family or a class of society that is considered a group of people that can be used for slavery.

- **Trafficking:** People are taken from one place and moved to another to be enslaved. Studies estimate that 70 percent of people trafficked are women and 50 percent are children.
- **Early and enforced marriage:** People, typically women, are forced to marry someone and to accept a life of servitude. In most cases, they have no way of leaving these marriages.
- **Child slavery:** Children are forced into labour and are trafficked. Approximately 5.5 million children are forced into child slavery and labour around the world.

servitude: *lack of freedom; having to serve and obey others*

A young boy tries to sell combs at a flea market in the Monastiraki neighbourhood of Athens.

CHILD LABOUR

Child slavery takes many forms. It often involves trafficking and enforced labour. Child labour is not always slavery. However, it does stop children from getting an education. It can negatively affect their mental and emotional growth. Around the world, there are over 200 million children working instead of going to school. Of these children, about 115 million do hazardous work. Hazardous work subjects a child to harmful working conditions, such as having to use dangerous machinery and being exposed to toxic substances.

Being a *restavek* is a form of modern-day slavery that affects children in Haiti. A *restavek* is a child who stays with a family and works in the family's house in exchange for food and a place to live. These children are often abused and cannot escape their situation. They face heavy emotional damage. Most do not go to school. Many cook, clean, and shop for the family, but are not treated as part of the family.

> Slavery continues to exist in North America, Eastern Europe, and other countries around the world. Many children forced into slavery live in North Korea, Afghanistan, Myanmar, and Somalia.

Haiti is an extremely impoverished country. After Haiti gained independence, Haitians were asked to pay France a tax for their independence. Approximately 80 percent of people in rural Haiti live in poverty. Due to high rates of poverty and high birth rates in rural communities, many rural children are born into families that are unable to provide for them. The only solution that some families see is to send children to live with families in the city. But these urban families are also facing many financial problems. They often have to put the children to work in order to be able to accept them into their homes. This is how children become *restaveks*.

A child labourer working in a family's home

Children attending a school

RESTAVEK FREEDOM

Restavek Freedom was started in 2007. The people who work there are parents, students, volunteers, community leaders, and reporters. It is located in Port-au-Prince and Port Salut, Haiti, and has a small support staff in Ohio, United States.

> Why is it important that the main staff of Restavek Freedom be located in Haiti?

According to Restavek Freedom, one out of 15 children in Haiti are *restaveks*.

Restavek Freedom's main goal is to help *restaveks* gain freedom. Restavek Freedom also aims to change governmental laws to better protect these children.

Restavek Freedom has started several programs, including literacy programs and programs for women's groups, which provide job training and teach life skills. As well, Restavek Freedom hosts open community meetings that encourage families to talk with one another, offer support, and find ways of helping their children other than sending them away. Restavek Freedom is not about blaming families. It is about helping them change a situation that hurts everyone.

CONNECT IT

Using the Internet, do some research to find out more about Restavek Freedom. Create a pamphlet to encourage people to support the organization. Be sure to explain why this is an important cause for achieving freedom for these children.

Interview With
Kevan Anthony Cameron
a.k.a. Scruffmouth

KEVAN ANTHONY CAMERON, a.k.a. Scruffmouth, is a writer and performance poet. He is the author of six chapbooks (small, pocket sized booklets). He has also produced several CDs and co-edited *The Great Black North: Contemporary African Canadian Poetry* with Valerie Mason-John. He graduated with a Bachelor of Arts degree from Simon Fraser University in 2003. In the following interview by Adrienne Shadd, Scruffmouth talks about finding his voice and freedom through his art.

Adrienne Shadd: First of all, tell me where you live and a bit about your background.

Scruffmouth: I live in Burnaby, British Columbia. I was born in Edmonton, Alberta, and I grew up in Sherwood Park, Alberta. My parents immigrated to Canada from Jamaica. Education, sports, music, and the arts were important aspects of my growth and development from childhood to adulthood.

immigrated: *moved from one country to another*

AS: Where did the name Scruffmouth come from?

S: Scruffmouth was a name my brother gave me in high school when he was teasing me about my facial hair.

AS: What made you decide to become a writer and performance poet?

S: I was always interested in writing. When I started attending poetry slams in my last year at university, I knew spoken word was something I could get into that would be an outlet for my writing, as well as a way to use my voice. I decided to become a writer and performance poet when I realized how powerful these art forms were for myself and others.

> Poetry slams are competitions where people perform their own poetry. Audience members decide who gave the best performance and that person is the winner.

AS: Why do you say these art forms are so powerful?

S: I was always an avid reader when I was growing up and in grade 3, I wrote a short story called "Chickens on Strike" for the County of Strathcona anthology *Stepping Stones*. In grade 5, when we studied poetry in class, we were directed to write about something we were passionate about. I chose to write a poem on sleep, appropriately called "Sleep," and received a 5 out of 5. Language Arts was always a central subject for me in school because the skills you develop are applied to other subjects. The process of reading, thinking, and writing is always happening in some order. Most people have a fear of public speaking. But fears should not prevent you from empowering yourself with knowledge. When I learned to use my voice, I realized that I was not only helping myself by speaking up, but I was also voicing the thoughts and opinions for others.

> How can knowledge empower you and help you achieve personal freedom?

After I graduated from university, I was attending the Vancouver Poetry Slam and listening to poets speak their truth onstage. It seemed similar to a university lecture, but instead of three hours, lessons were condensed into three minutes, just like a song or a music video. After taking a season off soccer due to injury, I found the time, space, and need to express my knowledge in an art form that was interesting and uplifting. This is when I realized the word, sound, and power of poetry.

AS: Have you published any books?

S: I have self-published several chapbooks and co-edited an anthology of contemporary African Canadian poetry entitled *The Great Black North*.

AS: What are the themes or topics you like to write about?

S: Knowledge of self, history, identity, philosophy, artistic expression, creative genius, social justice, freedom, spirituality, and relationships are all themes and topics that I enjoy writing about and that are important to me. They represent who I am at the core of my being and serve to create thought and a sense of awareness for the reader and listener.

AS: Recently you recited a poem in which you quoted the popular African proverb "Until the lion becomes a scholar, history will be written by the hunter." Can you talk about this poem, and can you expand on your writing about the freedom of Black people?

S: It is important for Black people to tell their own stories so that we can know who we are and where we came from. Some of our story is passed down from generation to generation by word of mouth, which is known as the oral tradition. These traditions continue to this day through dub poetry, rap music, hip-hop culture, and spoken word. An exercise of freedom is creative expression and the ability to create art forms that serve yourself and others. The lion has a responsibility to share his stories with his entire pride. If the lion tells his pride the story written by the hunter, all the lion is doing is preparing his pride to be hunted and killed. But if the lion tells his own story of being king of the jungle, then he is preparing his pride to be kings, queens, and royalty.

proverb: *common, brief saying that expresses a wise opinion*

> Why is the publication of books such as *The Great Black North* important in fighting discrimination against African Canadians?

> In what ways would stories told by a hunter differ from those told by a lion?

AS: You mentioned that people have a fear of public speaking. Has it been difficult for you to go in front of an audience and recite your poems?

S: Yes and no. Yes because, as I said, public speaking is a common fear. No because I am compelled to use my voice. The decision to abandon my shyness and overcome my fear of getting my thoughts off my chest was a simple decision to leave my comfort zone so I could challenge myself with the experience of sharing my knowledge.

AS: I understand that you are involved in a group called Black Dot Roots and Culture Collective. What does this group do, and what is your role in the group?

S: Black Dot Roots and Culture Collective is a group of artists and professionals that program events, activities, and festivals that showcase the educational, creative, and celebratory aspects of the Black experience of peoples of African descent. I am the creative director.

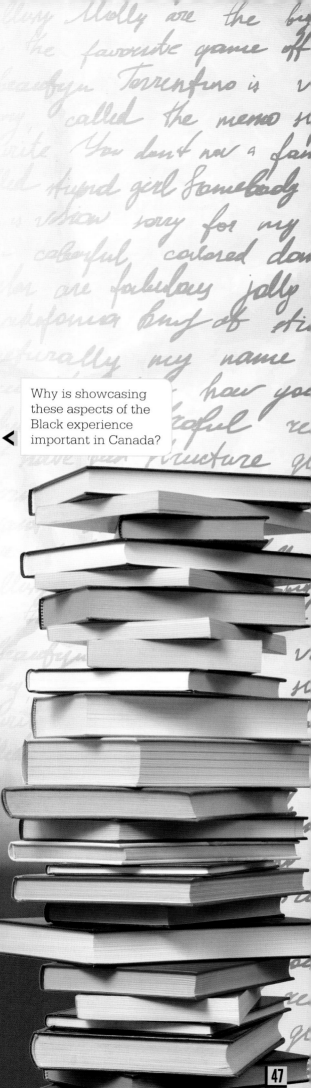

Why is showcasing these aspects of the Black experience important in Canada?

AS: What other things do you do? Do you have any other interests?

S: I play and coach soccer, work in the film and television industry, and collect comic books and graphic novels. I am interested in travelling and discovering new adventures.

AS: What advice would you give young people who want to become writers and do what you do?

S: Go and experience the world you live in. Read a lot and take the path less travelled.

CONNECT IT

Scruffmouth not only writes about freedom, but he also uses poetry as a way to free himself of his shyness. In a small group, talk about how the arts play an important role in promoting the message of freedom. What creative format would you use to share your feelings (poetry, stories, songs, artwork, etc.)?

Index

Acknowledgements

The publisher gratefully acknowledges the following for permission to reprint copyrighted material in this book.

Angelou, Maya. "Caged Bird," from *Shaker, Why Don't You Sing?* by Maya Angelou, copyright © 1983 by Maya Angelou. Used by permission of Random House, an imprint and division of Random House LLC. All rights reserved.

Sirleaf, Ellen Johnson. "A Voice for Freedom." Copyright © The Nobel Foundation (2011) Source: Nobelprize.org

"Detroit River Frontier & John 'Daddy' Hall." Permission courtesy of The Harriet Tubman Institute for Research on the Global Migrations of African Peoples.

Ruggles, Clifton. "Liberation Forces: Excerpt of "Remembering the other forgotten solider," by Clifton Ruggles from *Some Missing Pages: The Black Community in the History of Quebec and Canada*. Permission courtesy of the Quebec Board of Black Educators.

Cooper, Afua. "Hired Out." Material from *My Name is Henry Bibb: A Story of Slavery and Freedom* by Afua Cooper is used by permission of Kids Can Press Ltd., Toronto, Canada. Text © 2009 Afua Cooper. As Provided.

Photo Sources
Cover: Mandela–catwalker/Shutterstock.com; **4:** sunset–Carlos Violda/Shutterstock.com; **6:** [bird–Anna Paff; cage–nikit_a] Shutterstock.com; **7:** [tree branch–Emir Simsek; bird 2–Anna Paff] Shutterstock.com; **8:** [linen background–Kazarlenya; woven banner texture–White Room] Shutterstock.com; ships carrying Black captives–DeAgostini / SuperStock; first African slaves–©North Wind Picture Archives; **9:** Emancipation parade–Library and Archives Canada/PA-163923; Harriet Tubman–Library of Congress; Richard Pierpoint–Illustration by Malcolm Jones © Canadian War Museum; Henry Bibb–Bentley Historical Library; Egerton Ryerson–Government of Ontario Art Collection; **10:** Mary Ann Shadd–National Archives of Canada, C-029977; Emancipation Proclamation–Library of Congress; school group–Archives of Ontario, I0024782; brotherhood of sleeping car porters–Everett Collection / SuperStock; **11**: A Fair Employment Practices Committee–National Archives; Michaëlle Jean–David Prichard/GlowImages.com; Lincoln Alexander–Tony Bock / GetStock.com; Jean Augustine–Charla Jones / GetStock.com; Universal Declaration of Human Rights–United Nations, New York; **12:** blue paper rip– Nicolas Raymond/Shutterstock.com; John Daddy Hall–Grey Roots Museum & Archives; **13:** Bombardment Of Fort Detroit–P_Rindlisbacher; The Meeting of Brock–Library and Archives of Canada; **14:** wood–CrazyLazy/Shutterstock.com; corn-shucking–Library of Congress; **16:** shucking–Library of Congress; **17:** Voice of Fugitive–Library and Archives Canada; **18:** chestnut tree–T. Kimmeskamp/Shutterstock.com; **19:** Viola Desmond–Marsha Barrow Smith; newspaper–R. Cherubin/Shutterstock.com; **20:** deck–Symbiot/Shutterstock.com; **22:** flags–mattasbestos/Shutterstock.com; Band Parade–Courtesy of North Buxton National Historic Site and Museum, Courtesy of Adrienne Shadd; **23:** Maple Leaf Forever–Alexander Muir (1830-1906); [picture frame–Microstock Man; drums–Milosz Aniol] Shutterstock.com; **25:** drum sticks–Dmitry Veryovkin/Shutterstock.com; band members–Courtesy of Adrienne Shadd; **26:** purple–antishock/Shutterstock.com; Nobel Peace Prize Winners–©ZUMAPRESS.com/Keystone Press; **28:** Ellen Johnson Sirleaf–© Roger Fosaas/Stella/ZUMAPRESS.com; **29:** crowd–© Ahmed Jallanzo/UPPA/ZUMAPRESS.com; **30:** Mandela–TREVOR SAMSON/AFP/Getty Images; **32:** jail–© David Turnley/Corbis; **33:** Sowetto crowd–PHILIP LITTLETON/AFP/GettyImages; **30:** static noise background–Simeon Chatzilidis/Shutterstock.com; **35:** background–Perfect Vectors/Shutterstock.com; [Martin Luther King; demonstrators] Library of Congress; **36:** crowd–Everett Collection / SuperStock; **38:** musical band–Harold E. Wright, Heritage Resources; poppies background–Sergieiev/Shutterstock.com; **39:** soldiers playing–© Bettmann/CORBIS; **40:** [scissors–Ingvar Bjork; wrench–Patryk Michalski; spool & buttons–Nattika; background–vata; kid carrying wood–paul prescott] Shutterstock.com; **41:** market background–lornet/Shutterstock.com; kid holding brush–JAMESON ZED/SIPA/Newscom; **42:** [girl–arindambanerjee; pots background–arindambanerjee; girls in school–arindambanerjee] Shutterstock.com; **44:** Scruffmouth–courtesy of Kevan Anthony Cameron, Adrienne Shadd, [writing background–Svetlana Prikhnenko; texture background–foxie] Shutterstock.com; **46:** crowd & mic–wellphoto/Shutterstock.com; **47:** books pile–ajt/Shutterstock.com.